Christmas Treasury

A Holiday Gift of Memories

by Jerianne Van Dijk

HAVOC PUBLISHING

6330 Nancy Ridge Drive, Suite 104

San Diego, California 92121

For:

_____

Have Yourself a
Merry Little Christmas

Contents

Contents

Heralding the Holidays

The weeks before _____

_____

_____

_____

Reservations and special plans _____

_____

_____

_____

Invitations _____

_____

_____

Memorable Preparations

A Cup of Good Cheer

Parties to remember _____

_____

_____

_____

_____

A toast to _____

_____

_____

_____

_____

_____

Photos

Favorite recipes

Favorite recipes

Feast for the Eyes

Traditional meals

_____

_____

_____

_____

_____

_____

_____

_____

_____

_____

_____

_____

Photos

Photos

Traditional Treats

_____

_____

_____

_____

_____

_____

_____

_____

_____

_____

_____

_____

_____

Favorite recipes

_____

_____

_____

_____

_____

_____

_____

Favorite recipes

_____

_____

_____

_____

_____

_____

_____

Be Our Guest

Special visits _____

_____

_____

_____

_____

Memorable visitors _____

_____

_____

_____

_____

_____

Photos

The Tales of Our Times

A Christmas story shared _____

_____

_____

_____

_____

_____

_____

_____

_____

Treasured holiday readings _____

_____

_____

_____

_____

_____

Traditional television specials and movies

_____

_____

_____

_____

_____

News From Friends

Favorite Cards

_____

_____

_____

_____

_____

_____

_____

_____

Favorite Christmas stamps

place here

Photos

Photos

Sights and Lights

Pageants _____

_____

Parades _____

_____

Performances _____

_____

_____

_____

Events in our town _____

_____

_____

_____

The best decorations _____

_____

The brightest lights _____

_____

The most unique decorations _____

_____

Photo

Photos

Photos

Traditions Old and New

Each year...

_____

_____

_____

_____

_____

_____

_____

This year...

_____

_____

_____

_____

_____

Photos

Sounds of the Season

Favorite carols _____

_____

_____

_____

_____

Some new songs _____

_____

_____

_____

Holiday Vacations

Longest trip _____

_____

_____

Most interesting destination _____

_____

_____

_____

Favorite vacation getaway _____

_____

_____

_____

Memorable Vacation Story

Photos

Photos

Joy to the World

Local events _____

_____

_____

_____

National events _____

_____

_____

World events _____

_____

_____

Photos

Shopping and Dropping

Shopping pals _____

_____

Best purchase _____

_____

Most difficult find _____

_____

Last minute ideas _____

_____

_____

Last shopping day _____

Photos

'Tis the Season to Give

Acts of kindness _____
_____
_____
_____
_____

Gifts of love _____
_____
_____
_____

Most memorable gift given _____
_____

Most memorable gift received _____
_____

Photos

Holiday Crafts

New ideas _____
_____
_____
_____
_____

Old favorites _____
_____
_____
_____
_____
_____
_____
_____

Deck the Halls

Special decorations _____

_____

Favorite ornaments _____

_____

Tree topper _____

_____

Best Christmas tree _____

_____

_____

Funniest Christmas tree _____

_____

_____

Photos

Photos

'Twas the Night
Before Christmas

Photos

Christmas Day

A time to remember _____

_____

_____

_____

_____

_____

_____

_____

_____

_____

_____

_____

_____

_____

_____

Christmas Day

Photos

Holiday Afternoons

New games _____
_____
_____
_____

Old and new friends _____
_____
_____

Playful stories _____
_____
_____
_____
_____
_____

Photos

Photos

Photos

Photos

Photos

Out with the Old, In with the New

Each year... _____

_____

_____

_____

_____

_____

_____

This year... _____

_____

_____

_____

_____

Photos

New Year's Day

Resolutions _____

_____

_____

_____

_____

_____

Games, parades and friends _____

_____

_____

_____

_____

Photos

Photos

Photos

Things to be Thankful For

Angels to remember... _____
_____
_____
_____
_____
_____

Hopes for the year to come _____
_____
_____
_____
_____
_____
_____
_____

Photos

Available Record Books From Havoc

Baby

Coach

College Life

Couples

Dad

Girlfriends

Golf

Grandmother

Grandparents

Mom

Mothers & Daughters

My Pregnancy

Our Honeymoon

Retirement

School Days

Single Life

Sisters

Teacher

Traveling Adventures

Tying the Knot

Christmas Treasury

Home for the Holidays

haVoc
PUBLISHING